Proverbs For the Family

By Bruce Lackey

Published with the Permission of
Mrs. Helen Lackey, widow, through the ministry of Dr.
Bob Green
ISBN: 979-8-9857165-6-6
By The Old Paths Publications
TOP@theoldpathspublications.com
www.theoldpathspublications.com

Table of Contents

Introduction

The book of Proverbs is preeminently a book of the family. There are fifty-four references to it, in the thirty-one chapters which comprise this portion of scripture. Twenty-three times, the writer begins his remarks with the words, "My son." Because of the many forces which are at work to destroy the family in this age, and because some of the efforts of Christians to strengthen the family seem to be based primarily on the psychology of the world, it is imperative that we come again to God's eternal wisdom to learn His plan for the family.

May He give us the desire to do so, along with the Holy Spirit to enlighten the eyes of our understanding, enabling us to apply these principles to our situations.

Chapter 1

The Husband

> 5:15, "Drink waters out of thine own cistern, and running waters out of thine own well."

The husband is to be faithful to his one wife throughout his life. Solomon learned the miseries of not doing this and described them for us in Ecclesiastes 7:26-28:

"And I find more bitter than death the woman, whose heart is snares and nets, and her hands as bands: whoso pleaseth God shall escape from her; but the sinner shall be taken by her. Behold, this have I found, saith the preacher, counting one by one, to find out the account: Which yet my soul seeketh, but I find not: one man among a thousand have I found; but a woman among all those have I not found."

Among his seven hundred wives and three hundred concubines, he could not find a woman who would be true to him; he found only those whose hearts were "snares and nets, and her hands as bands." He tacitly confessed himself as a sinner who had not pleased God when he said, "the sinner shall be taken by her." After these bitter experiences, he gave good advice, which he surely wished that he himself had followed, in Eccl. 9:9:

> "Live joyfully with the wife whom thou lovest all the days of the life of thy vanity, which he hath given thee under the sun, all the days of thy vanity . . ."

We note that he said, "the wife," not the wives! Also, he emphasized that this should be a life-long commitment, by twice saying that this should be done "all the days of the life of thy vanity."

If we look at these words merely from the human standpoint, forgetting inspiration for the moment, we should see the wisdom of heeding this man's advice which he had learned from years of experience with a thousand wives. It is always a wise man who learns at someone else's expense. Then when we remember that all scripture is inspired and profitable (II Tim. 3: 16), these "words which the Holy Ghost teacheth" are potent and binding.

Ephesians 5:25-33 teaches the same thing: a man is to be faithful to his one wife, just as Christ is to His one bride, the church.

When the Lord said that the husband should "drink waters out of (his) own cistern," (Prov. 5: 15), He was teaching that the man should not only be faithful, but satisfied. He continues that in verses 18-19:

> ". . . rejoice with the wife of thy youth. Let her be as the loving hind and pleasant roe; let her breasts satisfy thee at all times; and be thou ravished always with her love."

The idea of satisfaction is obvious. It implies that the man should guard against any outside influence which would make him think of the possibility that another woman might be more enjoyable. Many a man has made the serious mistake of comparing his wife to some actress or model which he has seen in the movies, or on television, or in magazines, forgetting that they are indeed **acting.** No wonder the scripture warns us against the "lust of the eyes" (1 John 2: 15-16)!

That satisfaction is vitally connected with the physical relationship. Even the psychologists of the world have learned that a person's mental attitude toward the other determines whether or not the physical relationship is satisfactory and wholesome. God put that in His word centuries ago!

Also, that satisfaction is to be continued even in old age. Note the words "the wife of thy youth" in v. 18, and the words "at all times ... always" in v. 19.

Why would a man presumptuously embrace a stranger, knowing that the Lord sees it all? "And why wilt thou, my son, be ravished with a strange woman, and embrace the bosom of a stranger? For the ways of man are before the eyes of the LORD, and he pondereth all his goings." (vv. 20-21)

How is all this possible? Simply by thinking toward the wife as God teaches us in this pasBage. The way a man thinks will determine the way he acts; "as he thinketh in his heart, so is he," (23:7). This requires that a man know what God has said, make a commitment to obey it, and continually remind himself through the years to continue that obedience.

What are the benefits of such a commitment? Not only the obvious one of pleasing God by obeying His Word, but also that of having children who are a blessing to mankind, as rivers of waters are to thirsty land.

> "Let thy fountains be dispersed abroad, and rivers
> of waters in the streets." (v. 16)

The fact that this verse refers to children is seen by the Lord's use of similar language in other verses, describing children as waters from a source and as playing in the streets. See Isa. 48:1; Hos. 13:15; and Zech. 8:5. Also, the word **fountain** refers to the wife, in Lev. 20:18.

When husband and wife are faithful to each other, they also have the joy of knowing that these children, which are as rivers of water to a thirsty land, are their own!

> "Let thy fountains be dispersed abroad, and rivers of

waters in the streets." (v. 16.

Another commitment which the husband must make regards that which is his priority in the home, as we learn from 15: 16-1 7:

> "Better is little with the fear of the LORD than great treasure and trouble therewith. Better is a dinner of herbs where love is, than a stalled ox and hatred therewith."

The young man is pressured from all sides to succeed, and by that word, the world means to make more money and possess more things. If this becomes his priority, he faces the possibility of letting his work cause him to neglect his family; he could also be tempted to be dishonest in order to achieve them. To prevent these from happening, the Lord stresses two priorities in the above verses: the fear of the Lord, and love.

The fear of the Lord will keep a man from dishonesty; loving his wife will keep him from neglecting her. How simple all this sounds, and yet how very practical it is! Everyone knows that the family is being destroyed largely by greed and neglect. God showed us how to prevent that from happening, centuries ago, in these verses.

All of this implies that a choice must be made. It would be well for a man and woman to make these choices before the marriage, so that they both know what their priorities will be. What if we were to spend as much time and effort on learning the fear of God, and loving each other, as we spend on making money? It is easy to see that such would produce happy, spiritual marriages.

> "Whoso findeth a wife findeth a good thing, and obtaineth favour of the LORD." (18:22)

A man should seek a wife, not the other way around! A man should beware, when a woman "makes a play" for him. That could be the wrong kind of woman. Even though this may sound old-fashioned, the clear implication of this verse is that the man should seek a wife. Of course, involved in this would be the man praying that God would guide him to the right woman to be his wife, and the woman doing likewise. The implication here is that the two are already following the Lord.

Obviously, this verse was not intended to teach that every marriage is a blessing of God. Some marriages are most unpleasant, as seen from 19:13 ("the contentions of a wife are a continual dropping") and 25:24 ("It is better to dwell in the comer of the housetop, than with a brawling woman and in a wide house."). The verse describes the ideal, to which there are obvious exceptions. We must remember that Proverbs was written to teach us wisdom, etc. (1: 1-6), not to describe every situation in the world. There are several verses in Proverbs which must be considered in this way; they describe the ideal situation, not every situation. As an example, let us consider 16:7:

> "When a man's ways please the LORD, he
> maketh even his enemies to be at peace with him."

There have been obvious exceptions to this, not only in biblical times, but also in church history. Daniel and the three Hebrew children are notable examples of those who pleased the Lord, but had to suffer at the hands of their enemies. Even though these men were eventually delivered, there were other godly people through the ages who were not; see Heb. 11:35-40.

Charles Bridges, in his commentary on Proverbs, made a wise comment on this verse: "the man of God ... will always have his enemies, if from no other source, from 'his own household.' (Mat 10:36). To seek peace with them by compromise of principle, would be to forfeit his character at a dreadful cost. Let him hold fast his principles in the face of his enemies."

Rather than describing every situation in the world, this verse encourages us to please the Lord, by describing the reward of so doing. It was written "to give subtilty to the simple, to the young man knowledge and discretion," (1 :4). The same is true of 18:22; the implication is that the man has already learned to fear the Lord, as the previous chapters have instructed him, and that he is trusting in the Lord with all his heart, not leaning to his own understanding; in all his ways he is acknowledging him, expecting him to direct his paths (3 :5-6).

If such is true, the Lord will guide the man to His choice of a wife, and so the man will indeed "obtain favor of the Lord." It is wise for the man to remember this, when the inevitable times come that his wife displeases him in some way. Since we are still human, with the problems of the old nature, we can certainly expect to have problems with each other. Husbands and wives do displease each other; the problem comes when those instances are not treated in a scriptural way. When the wife displeases the husband, it will help him to forgive and/or tolerate her, if he remembers that she is God's favor to him! The longer we associate with one another, the more characteristics we see about the other person which we do not like. Some of those characteristics will never change; they are inherently part of the personality. There is a great need for a lot of tolerance, in this matter of human relationships, especially in marriage. That is why Eph. 4:2 tells us to forbear (tolerate) one another in love, being kind, tenderhearted, forgiving one another, even as God for Christ's sake has forgiven us (4:32).

Quite similar to this verse is 19: 14:

"House and riches are the inheritance of fathers; and a prudent wife is from the LORD."

A man should seek a prudent wife from the Lord, not from educational institutions, or social standing. Also, it is more important to have a prudent wife than a beautiful one (that is, if a choice must be made!). It is far too easy for a young man to be dazzled by physical beauty and not be able to see beyond it. We will probably never be able to escape the magnetism of physcial beauty, but a young man had better associate with that beautiful girl long enough to find out whether she has any prudence, or not. After the marriage takes place, those mundane, daily responsibilities of paying the bills and keeping house can have a lot of influence on the happiness of the couple.

Suppose a man finds out, after the marriage, that his wife is not prudent? This, along with other deficiencies, can certainly be corrected by obeying the principles which are taught in Proverbs. Prudence can be learned. Both man and wife should seek the wisdom of scripture and pray, believingly, that the Lord will give it. He promised to do so, in such verses as James 1:5, "If any of you lack wisdom, let him ask of God, that giveth to all men liberally, and upbraideth not; and it shall be given him."

Two other verses showing a man what kind of wife to seek are 21:9 & 19:

> "It is better to dwell in a corner of the housetop, than with a brawling woman in a wide house . . . It is better to dwell in the wilderness, than with a contentious and an angry woman."

A man's wife has far more influence on his happiness than his material possessions. So, he should spend more time choosing the right wife than in providing a house. To find her, it would be necessary to observe her under various circumstances. Then it would be easy to see whether she is a "brawler, or angry, or contentious."

Verse 9 is so important that it is repeated in 25:24. If a man ignores these warnings, he will find out the truth of 30:23; the earth is disquieted for an odious woman when she is married!

Once again, we see the wisdom of a long courtship, carried on under various circumstances, so that both man and woman can observe each other and discern the other's character traits.

If any of the characteristics which have been discussed in this chapter are missing in a marriage, there is still hope. There is always hope in God! He is described as "the God of hope" in Rom. 15: 13. A man can search the scriptures and pray about his own faults. God is certainly more interested in our improvement, than we are. He will hear and teach and enable the heart which is seeking Him. A husband can pray about his wife's needs, also. We should never give up on people. The God of Calvary loves sinners and is still perfectly capable of changing them today. He always uses His Word, a good example, and believing prayers. A man's responsibility, therefore, is to be right, himself, according to the scripture, and to believe God in prayer.

If we give up and take the world's way out, we are simply saying that the Bible is not true, or that we are not willing to get right with God so that He can hear our prayers. Let us obey God's instructions for ourselves, believe Him, and prove His promises in prayer!

Chapter 2

The Wife

The wife has a greater influence on the atmosphere of the home than any other. Many of the instructions to the husband imply some things about the wife. For instance, let's consider 5: 15-21.

Verse 15, "Drink waters out of thine own cistern, and running waters out of thine own well," implies that the waters are there to drink; that is, that the wife is trying to be a satisfying companion to her husband. Just as drinking water is absolutely necessary to the physical well-being of the body, and is a very satisfying experience to the thirsty one, so the physical relationship of husband and wife are absolutely necessary to the well-being of the marriage. Not only should the husband be faithful to his wife and seek all his satisfaction with her, but also the wife should be one whose company is satisfying. Efforts must be made on the part of both.

The same truth implied in verse 18, "... rejoice with the wife of thy youth." The wife must be the kind in whom her husband can rejoice. And this characteristic should continue in old age, so that the rejoicing is there as it was in youth. Everyone knows that the initial physical attraction, along with the novelty of it, soon becomes commonplace. The correct mental attitude toward the physical relationship is vital, if it is to be a satisfying one. Even the marriage counselors of the world recognize this and are continually advising husbands and wives to think in certain ways before engaging in it.

When God instructed the wife, in Eph. 5:22-24, to be submissive to her husband, He did not mean for that to be a passive or mechanical submission. If we remember that the comparison of the husband-wife relationship is made to that of Christ and the church, we will realize that the wife's submission is to be joyful and active, even as the church is supposed to follow Christ.

The question of verse 20, "And why wilt thou, my son, be ravished with a strange woman, and embrace the bosom of a stranger," implies that such would be unnecessary and foolish, if the man were satisfied with his wife. Then, verse 21 is a reminder that God sees the actions and attitudes of both husband and wife, when it says "For the ways of man are before the eyes of the LORD, and he pondereth all his goings."

> "A virtuous woman is a crown to her husband: but she that maketh ashamed is as rottenness in his bones." (12:4)

God's purpose, when He created the woman, was that she would be a helper to her husband (Gen. 2:18). It would be just the opposite if she were "as rottenness in his bones." To be a helper, "a crown to her husband," she would have to be virtuous. The virtuous woman is described in detail in 31:1o-31; see the comments on this passage at the end of this chapter.

If a wife makes her husband ashamed of her, it hurts him on the inside, "as rottenness in the bones." Inner pain is the very worst kind. And, if it is like rottenness in the bones, it is incurable. While a man may forgive, he can never forget a wife who shamed him. We may condemn this as the wrong attitude, but it is a fact, nevertheless. Therefore, we have this admonition for the wife to avoid being that kind.

How much better it is to be the crown on his head, than merely the ring on his finger! What distinguishes the king from the pauper? The king's crown. When does a man become a king? When he is crowned. A virtuous wife's place is one of dignity; it is also obvious to everyone. And a virtuous wife's influence on her husband is without equal. What compares to a king's crown?

> "Every wise woman buildeth her house: but the foolish plucketh it down with her hands." (14:1)

The *house* may be the building, as it is in 5:8 & 7:6, or it may be the family, as in 15:27 & Psa. 135:19-20. Regarding the wife's place in her family, more will be said in the chapter on the mother. With respect to her responsibility toward building a house, 31: 16, 18, 24 show that she should have a financial part in it. More will be said in the discussion of those verses at the end of this chapter. Here, the idea seems to be that of conservation and wise use of possessions, rather than being wasteful. The wise builds (contributes); the foolish plucks down (wastes). In our day of wealth, it is sometimes difficult to draw the line between necessity and luxury. We need wisdom from the Lord in this, as in all other decisions. This verse gives us a principle by which we can make decisions. We should avoid extravagances which will plunge us into debt and result in the loss of the house.

The Christian can trust the Lord to provide a place to live, because in Phil. 4: 19, He promised to supply all our needs. That may be a rented house, or one that is owned, according to His will; in either case, the wife should avoid buying or even wanting those things which are going to require such expense or debt as to cause them to lose their place of residence. How often people spend their substance for gadgets which they move from place to place, but never have their own place to put them!

> "Better is little with the fear of the LORD than great treasure and trouble therewith. Better is a dinner of

herbs where love is, than a stalled ox and hatred
therewith." (15:16-17)

See the remarks on these verses in chapter 1, on the husband. The emphasis here is on priorities; for the young couple, they should be (I) the fear of the Lord and (2) love. Please refer to chapter one.

"The LORD will destroy the house of the proud:
but he will establish the border of the widow." (15:25)

When we are young, it is difficult for us to make provision for either old age or tragedy, but this verse implies that a woman should think ahead and attempt to be the kind of Christian who can claim this promise. There is a distinct possibility of widowhood and it could come at any time. Preparations should be made.

The fact that this verse is not a description of every situation in the world should be obvious. There are exceptions to it, as there are to other verses in Proverbs. This book was not written to describe every person or situation in the world, but "to give subtilty to the simple, to the young man knowledge and discretion," (I :4). The implication here is that the person who would claim this promise has also tried to obey the commands of the previous chapters. That implication is found in I :5, "A wise man will hear, and will increase learning." The idea of progressive hearing and obedience is obvious. The same idea is found in 9:9. We cannot expect to jump into the middle of Proverbs, find a promise, then expect God to keep it, while at the same time we i$_{g\,n}$ore the other verses in the book which give us instruction!

Therefore if a woman would expect the Lord to provide for her in the event of tragedy, she should seek to obey the commands and live by the principles of this book. Such a widow could expect the Lord to establish her border. That obedience would not only include the "spiritual" things herein, but the "practical" ones also, such as those which speak of honesty and thrift. There is much in this book about the wise use of money. See the topical arrangements of verses in the latter part of this volume.

The comments above would apply here, also; this verse does not describe every single marriage in the world, but that between two people who have been trying to live by these Proverbs. The clear implication is that the man has sought the woman, not the other way around. That does not mean that a woman is helpless and must be entirely passive in the matter of marriage. It seems clear that her responsibility is to be the kind of wife which is approved, here in Proverbs; if such is true, she can expect the Lord to fulfill His promise in 3:5-6 and "direct her paths." If she is obeying the Word and is trusting the Lord for the right husband, He will surely honor that attitude. That kind of wife is a good thing to find; she is indeed a favor from the Lord. Surely, every Christian woman would want to be the Lord's favor to her husband, and would want her husband to consider her so. This is a promise that such will be true to the obedient Christian woman.

This is one of several verses which teach that the wife probably has the greatest influence on the happiness of the home. A wife will not be contentious (argumentative), if she concerns herself with obedience to the verses which are discussed in this chapter. For instance, she will not be contentious about the physical relationship, if she remembers 5: 15-21. She will not be contentious about not having what others have, if she remembers 14: 1 and 15: 16-17.

If a woman wants to be considered as a wife who was given to her husband by the Lord, she must set out early in life to learn prudence. The Hebrew word which is translated *prudent* here is rendered *wisdom* in 1:3, *instructed* in 21: 11, and *understanding* in 21: 16. Combining all this, we learn that to be prudent is to have wisdom and understanding, having been instructed by the Lord.

"It is better to dwell in a comer of the housetop, than with a brawling woman in a wide house." (21:9 & 25:24) "It is better to dwell in the wilderness, than with a contentious and an angry woman." (21 :19) "A continual dropping in a very rainy day and a contentious woman are alike. Whosoever hideth her hideth the wind, and the ointment of his right hand, which bewrayeth itself." (2 7: 15-16)

The unpleasant characteristics of a wife which cause misery in the home are described as brawling, being contentious (argumentative) and angry. Brawling implies the physical expression of anger and strife. Neither husband nor wife should attack the other, physically. The husband's pattern is Christ (Eph. 5:25-33), who corrects His bride but does not chastise her. Chastening is from the Father to His children (Heb. 12:7). There is no scriptural justification for wife-beating.

The wife's pattern is the church (Eph. 5:22-24), which is subject to Christ in all things.

It is impossible for a couple to hide their fighting from others. Trying to do so is like trying to conceal perfume which has been put on one's hand; it is impossible.

Christian couples must not allow fights or even disagreements to continue unchecked. Sooner or later, others will know about them and their Christian testimony will be destroyed. This would be especially important for those couples who have any place of leadership in church. The problem cannot be ignored, or considered to be unimportant. It must be resolved, or else the cause of Christ will be hindered.

> "For three things the earth is disquieted ... for an odious woman when she is married ..." (30:21, 23).

Again, emphasis is laid on preparation for marriage. If a woman does not become the kind which is described here in Proverbs, she will disturb the peace of the earth. The word *odious* is translated *enemy* in 25 :21; *foe* in Est. 9: 16; *hate* in Gen. 29: 10, and *hateful* in Psa. 36:2. Obviously all these are opposite to that which the Lord intended the wife to be: a helper to her husband.

No doubt, God put such verses as these in Proverbs to show that (1) the attitude of the wife is largely responsible for the happiness of the home, and (2) preparation must be made if a woman is to be the right kind of wife. What a responsibility this places on the young ladies, and on those who teach them!

The classic passage describing the virtuous woman, 31 :10-31, is no doubt the climax of all that· has been said about a good wife, in Proverbs. It is helpful to remember that these are the words of a woman (v. 1); if they are from Bathsheba to her son, Solomon, they are all the more arresting, considering her past and the way that God had worked in her heart.

> "Who can find a virtuous woman? For her price is far above rubies." (v. 10)

Realizing that Solomon would be rich, as David's successor, she instructed him that his wealth would not be able to buy a virtuous woman. The implication is that, if a woman were to marry primarily for money, she would not be virtuous. Something far more precious than rubies is required to get a virtuous woman for a wife. All that has been said in previous chapters about preparation for marriage is thus called to memory.

> "The heart of her husband doth safely trust in her,
> so that he shall have no need of spoil." (v.11)

The virtuous woman's husband has no need to suspect her, because she is trustworthy; not a flirt; not a "silly woman laden with sins" (II Tim. 3:6-7). She wears modest clothes (I Tim 2:9), that is, clothing which would not accentuate the sexual zones of the body; her husband can tell by her appearance that she is not trying to attract the attention of other men. She does not let the ungodly tell her how to dress; she does not wear something merely because it is in style, but considers how it will portray her and her relationship to her husband. She is chaste, obeying Titus 2:5 and I Pet. 3:2. She has learned to love her husband (Titus 2:4), making it obvious, so that her husband has no reason to suspect otherwise.

She is satisfied with what he provides and does not waste it, so that he has no need to leave home to pursue the soldier's spoils. (In Biblical days, there was virtually no middle class; people were either poor or rich. About the only honest way a poor man could get more than the meager necessities of life was to become a soldier, so that he could take the possessions of those he had defeated. This would have been his only possibility to "get spoils." The modern parallel would be for a man to take a second job, or otherwise neglect his family, simply because he had to have more money to please a nagging wife.)

"She will do him good and not evil all the days of her
life." (v.12)

How would a wife do her husband evil? Proverbs has
already given us some examples:

12:4, making him ashamed

14:1, plucking down the house (wasting)

19: 13, being argumentative

21 :9, brawling

21 :19, being angry

30:23, being his enemy

Other examples in scriptures are:

Gen. 3:6, Eve's tempting her husband to disobey
God.

I Kings 11 :1-5, Solomon's wives, turning his heart
away from God to idols

I Kings 21 :25, Jezebel, stirring up Ahab to
work wickedness in the sight of the LORD

In contrast to these ways of doing him evil, doing her
husband good is the subject of this paragraph, especially vv.
11-27.

"She seeketh wool, and flax, and worketh willingly
with her hands." (v. 13)

In those days, only the rich could afford to pay someone
to make their clothes; the poor had to make their own
(ready-made garments which are so common to us were all
but unknown to them. Thus, the soldiers were anxious to
appropriate the clothes of Jesus when he was crucified).
The virtuous woman is a willing worker; she does not think
that the world (or the government, or anyone else) owes her
a living. She does what is necessary to maintain the home.

While her husband may provide the money, she uses it wisely to secure the wool and flax necessary for the family's clothes.

Even in our day, when ready-made clothes are so easily available and when they are made with material which is so easy to wash and wear, it is wise for the virtuous woman to learn to make and alter clothes. This is especially necessary during times when fashionable clothes are immodest and godly women have a difficult time finding the proper things to wear.

> "She is like the merchants' ships; she bringeth her food from afar." (v. 14)

Her husband may provide the money, but she should procure the food. The idea of "bringing food from afar" implies that she is interested in getting food for her family which is sometimes above the ordinary, that is, "imported." Providing such shows an unusual care and desire for the loved ones to have the very best.

> "She riseth also while it is yet night, and giveth meat to her household, and a portion to her maidens." (v. 15)

This may describe the situation where the woman and her husband have prospered to the extent of having a family and, possibly, workers in their business. While her husband may supervise other parts of their affairs, she is responsible for the maidens. She is a diligent steward over their possessions and provides well for their workers.

> "She considereth a field, and buyeth it with the fruit of her hands she planteth a vineyard." (v. 16)

This virtuous woman is not treated as a possession, but has access to the finances of the family. She may be involved in business transactions, such as the purchase of property. The word *considereth* implies that she has had some training in such matters so that she is able to make wise decisions. It is certainly not wrong for a woman to get an education; in our day, it is almost imperative. An educated wife can be a tremendous asset to her husband, not only in financial matters, but also in relieving him of worry about her qualifications to manage the family possessions. She is also qualified to engage in helpful and pleasant conversation regarding their assets.

Verses 18 & 24 also show that the wife can be involved in business transactions. Thus we would conclude that it is not a sin for a wife to have a career, but we must be careful to note that, along with these business activities, most of the verses in the paragraph emphasize her responsibilities at home. If her career causes her to neglect her family duties, or makes it necessary for her to delegate them to others, she would be disobeying scripture. The wife's career should not take the place of her family responsibilities. Verses 14-15 have told us that it is she, not someone whom she appoints, who provides the food for the household. Verse 27 says that it is she who looks well to the ways of her household, not someone whom she appoints. The Lord will surely provide a godly woman such opportunities, if her desire is to follow His directions in scripture. Later, in the verses which speak of parental training, we will see that it is always wrong to neglect children; there is never an acceptable excuse. Circumstances may be difficult, but Phil. 4: 19 is still true and God will keep His promise; He will provide ways for the wife-mother to work, when necessary, which do not make her neglect her family responsibilities.

> "She girdeth her loins with strength, and strengtheneth her arms." (v. 17)

A godly woman should be concerned about her health, but not for the reasons that are so popular among unbelievers. The motive here is not to be more attractive physically, but to be stronger. Diets, exercise, and all the other "fads" which come our way should have a place in our lives only if they are for the right motive: to be stronger. The desire to be more attractive physically is full of danger. Of course, the proper diet and exercise which strengthens will also frequently make one look better, but this should not be the motive.

> "She perceiveth that her merchandise is good: her candle goeth not out by night." (v. 18)

The virtuous woman does quality work. She is not careless. The meals which she provides are both nutritious and delicious. The clothes that she makes are of the finest quality. All that she does is "for the glory of God," (I Cor. 10:31), hence she has given her very best and is a good testimony for Christ. God gets no glory from excuse-making, such as, "I haven't practiced much, but I'm doing this for the Lord, anyhow." If we really are doing something for the Lord, our efforts should be greater than those who do things for money, or for reputation! The virtuous woman's merchandise is good, and she knows it, because she has not wasted her time in night-revelry, but has used her moments well to achieve superiority.

This does not forbid times of relaxation, but does remind us that quality work is done by those who are not time wasters.

> "She layeth her hands to the spindle, and her hands hold the distaff." (v. 19)

A modern application would be that she has learned to work with her hands on such things as sewing machines, typewriters, pianos, computers, etc. None of this is meant to stereotype certain kinds of work, saying that only women may cook, or sew; rather these are given as examples to be considered. It is a wise woman who learns to work with her hands. Such a quality is rare, in our day, when so many labor-saving devices are available. If one looks for the opportunities, there are still many ways that a wife can become superior in working with her hands at various things. Not only would this enable her to contribute to the financial needs of the home, but it would also give her invaluable skills which may be needed in the event of her husband's becoming an invalid, or his death, or other financial strains. God's word, in describing virtue and godliness, is always practical.

This woman is not only trustworthy, industrious, strong, and a quality worker, she is also concerned about the needy. Perhaps one reason is that the foregoing qualities are true of an unselfish person. When people are selfish, they usually lack some or all of the above.

A good scriptural example of such a woman is Dorcas (Acts 9:36, 39).

This characteristic of concern for others is so important, that the Lord made it one of the qualifications of the widow who was to be "taken into the number" of the church at Ephesus (I Tim. 5:9). That phrase is interpreted by some to mean merely financial support, while others explain it to mean the hiring of a widow as a servant of the church to minister to the women and to the needy. Whatever the interpretation, the Lord made it clear that such a widow should be "taken into the number" only if she had "lodged strangers. . . .washed the saints' feet, . . . relieved the afflicted," (I Tim 5: 10).

Likewise, Christ commanded us to love one another as He loved us (John 15: 12). I Pet. 4:8 says it this way, "And above all things, have fervent charity among yourselves: for charity shall cover the multitude of sins." When we see the word *charity* in the New Testament, we should think of John 3:16. *Charity* comes from the same Greek word which is translated *loved,* in that verse. The translators used *charity* to emphasize that this love is a giving love; therefore, if we think of John 3: 16, we will be reminded to love as God loved, giving the very best, giving what is needed.

So we see that the description of the virtuous woman, in Prov. 31 :20, is not insignificant, but is a most important qualification throughout the scripture, especially to the person who would be like the Lord.

> "She is not afraid of the snow for her household: for all her household are clothed with scarlet." (v. 21)

It is virtuous to make preparation for the future! Some people have misunderstood Christ's words in Mat. 6: 19-34, that we should "take no thought for the morrow . . ." He was not condemning the common-sense preparation for the future that is a part of everyday life. He was speaking of the greed which makes a person lay up treasures for the future by disobeying the Lord. He made that clear when, right in the middle of the discourse, He said, "No man can serve two masters," (v. 24). That is the key; if my preparation for the future would make me disobey the Lord, it would be a sin. However, if it does not interfere with my doing the will of God, there is nothing wrong with it. The Lord, Himself, told the disciples to make certain preparations for the future, in Luke 22:35-36, "and he said unto them, When I sent you without purse, and scrip, and shoes, lacked ye any thing? And they said, Nothing. Then he said unto them, But now, he that hath a purse, let him take it, and likewise his scrip; and he that hath no sword, let him sell his garment, and buy one."

Also, in Prov. 13:22, the Lord has told us,

> "A good man leaveth an inheritance to his children's children."

Scholars tell us that scarlet was obtained from the kermes insect which feeds on a species of live oak. A little reflection on that would show us that much work was required to get enough dye to color clothes. In order to provide her household with scarlet, the virtuous woman would have to expend much time and effort. This is another evidence of her diligence and desire that her family have the very best.

> "She maketh herself coverings of tapestry; her clothing is silk and purple." (v. 22)

Since she has already shown her unselfishness by providing abundantly for her family and also for the poor, there is nothing wrong in her having beautiful clothes for herself. Tapestry, silk, and purple would have been costly, but this woman has already proved that she is not extravagant, especially in verses 11 & 20. It is not wrong for a trustworthy, industrious, charitable, thrifty woman to have beautiful and even costly clothes. God nowhere puts a premium on poverty. He does promise prosperity to those who are obedient to Him. This woman is an example that He honors those who honor Him, by being the kind of person who is obedient to scripture.

As further proof that she is not selfish or extravagant, we are told that she made these clothes herself. Once again we see evidence of her skill and work.

It is an honor for a man to have his wife be beautiful in appearance. It is an evidence of the blessing of God for the obedience Christian to show that He rewards those who follow the scripture.

> "Her husband is known in the gates, when he sitteth among the elders of the land." (v. 23)

A man can succeed when he has this kind of wife! He is happy at home; he is not worried about her unfaithfulness, nor her wastefulness, nor her idleness,. He is free of care about the welfare of the family because she has seen to it diligently. He has been able to apply himself to his career and his success is obvious to all.

> "She maketh fine linen, and selleth it; and delivereth girdles unto the merchant." (v. 24)

This, along with the previous discussions on verses 16 & 18, repeat the fact that the wife may be involved in making money. We note, again, the emphasis on her quality work, in the phrase "fine linen."

> "Strength and honour are her clothing; and she shall rejoice in time to come." (v. 25)

Even though she has tapestry, silk and purple for clothes (v. 22), the first thing that people notice about her is her strength and honor, not the kind of material she is wearing! She is not like the woman described in 11:22 ("As a jewel of gold in a swine's snout, so is a fair woman which is without discretion."). Her beauty is in her character and accomplishments, while at the same time she has a pleasing appearance.

Because her beauty is more than clothes, she shall rejoice in the time to come. She has already made preparation for the future (vv. 16 & 21), so it is her work that gives her such confidence and joy.

> "She openeth her mouth with wisdom; and in her tongue is the law of kindness." (v. 26)

A woman who has the characteristics of vv. 11-25 will also possess great wisdom. A person may learn facts in a school, but wisdom is learned from the application of those facts in the ways .which have been discussed in this paragraph. This woman has had training; she has learned to make clothes, prepare meals, purchase property, plant vineyards, engage in business, and plan for the future. Such a woman is worth listening to! In the verses which describe the mother, we will see that she is a vital part of the training of the children. Children would do well to heed the wisdom of such a wife and mother.

This wisdom is dispensed with kindness. In her dealings with her husband, her maidens, and the merchants, she has learned how to be kind in every possible circumstance. Rather than being arrogant toward those who have not yet attained those things which she has, she remembers that she, too, had to go through the process of learning, before she had the success which she now enjoys. Rather than being impatient with the poor and needy, she remembers when she, too, had few possessions, having to work with her own hands and plant her own vineyard.

When 1:8 admonishes the son to not forsake "the law of thy mother," this law of kindness is no doubt in mind.

> "She looketh well to the ways of her household, and
> eateth not the bread of idleness." (v. 27)

Perhaps the reason this verse is near the end of the paragraph is to remind us that, in all the works and achievements of this virtuous woman, she has not neglected her family. God always reminds us of our priorities, when he teaches us how to succeed in life.

> "Her children arise up, and call her blessed; her
> husband also, and he praiseth her." (v. 28)

The reward of being a virtuous woman, as described in this paragraph, is the praise of her grown children and her successful husband. What a joy it is to know that one has contributed to the success and happiness of a whole family! Conversely, how many older women as well as men are bitter and sullen because they are reaping what they sowed for many years?

> "Many daughters have done virtuously, but thou excellest them all." (v. 29)

It is good to have "done virtuously," but it is infinitely better to be virtuous. Being virtuous excels doing virtuously. The quality of what one is excels what that one does. At the judgment seat of Christ, the fire shall try every Christian's work "of what sort it is," (I Cor. 3:13). He will also make manifest "the counsels of the hearts," (I Cor. 4:5). Without a doubt, God is more concerned with what we are, than what we do; He knows that what we are will determine the kinds of things we do, and the extent of their quality. It has often been said that man is looking for better methods, but God is looking for better men. That is true, also, of women. God is, indeed, looking for better women, so much so, that He has described in His Word just the kind of women which pleases Him, and which He is pleased to reward.

> "Favour is deceitful, and beauty is vain: but a woman that feareth the LORD, she shall be praised." (v. 30)

The reason the virtuous woman has been virtuous is that she fears the Lord. The fear of God is described in two places, in this book:

8:13, "The fear of the LORD is to hate evil." 16:6, "By

the fear of the LORD men depart from evil."

From these, we learn that the fear of the Lord is not that fear which makes one run away; it is not the cowardly kind. Rather, it makes one seek the Lord, desiring to forsake evil and obey Him. God has, again, reminded us that the virtuous woman does what she does, because she is what she is. The fear of the Lord is the great motive behind it all.

Because of it, she shall be praised, not only by her husband and children (v. 28), but by the Lord Himself, at the judgment seat of Christ (I Cor. 4:5).

> "Give her of the fruit of her hands; and let her own works praise her in the gates." (v. 31)

Perhaps this verse should more correctly be discussed in the chapter on husbands and children, since it is obviously an admonition to them. We should not wait for the judgment seat of Christ; we should do all within our power to praise the virtuous woman in this life. Without a doubt, she shall receive praise from her own accomplishments, if they are according to these verses.

When all the verses in this chapter are considered, a woman might consider them to be impossible in their requirements. That is often the reaction of a sincere Christian, when that Christian sees the big gap between what scripture requires and what we actually are. However, we can get the victory over such discouragement when we realize that God has not commanded us to do things which are beyond our ability. We can do all things through Christ, who strengthens us (Phil. 4: 13). Our responsibility is threefold: learn what the scripture has said, confess our failures, and strive to obey. Along with the apostle Paul, we can say that we have not yet apprehended, but we press toward the mark for the prize of the high calling of God in Christ Jesus (Phil. 3: 14).

The reward is worth it!

Chapter 3

Parents

"My son, hear the instruction of thy father, and forsake not the law of thy mother." (1:8)

Both father and mother are responsible to train the children, therefore, instead of having a chapter for the father and one for the mother, this chapter is for both. It is imperative that both father and mother agree and cooperate on matters of rearing children.

The father is to instruct; the mother is to have law. If the father instructs, he must have already learned these matters and have practiced them. A necessary part of instruction is example; pupils learn from seeing, more so than from being told. The topics about which the father is to instruct his children are right here in Proverbs. The part of this book which gives the topical arrangement of the verses should be helpful. It will be noticed that some topics, such as immorality, are discussed in several places. The reason for this is that God knows we need repetition; but repetition which is without variety is boring, so He has given us several places with different approaches which may be used for both repetition and interest.

It is a serious mistake for the father to leave all religious instruction up to the church, or to the Christian school. Of course, those institutions will be providing much of that, but there is no substitute for the personal instruction of a father.

It would be wise for the father to imitate God's example in his instruction. Rather than follow the same routine every time, he should seek variety, in the same way that God gives us several places discussing the same subject. Instruction which is varied will be more interesting and therefore more effective.

The family altar should not be turned into a lecture session. Instruction may be given, but we should remember always that it is a time of worship. Nothing should be done which would make the children dread it. Eph. 6:4 admonishes the fathers to "provoke not your children to wrath: but bring them up in the nurture and admonition of the Lord." If we know of something that is having a negative effect on the children, we should make an effort to change it. That is not to decrease discipline; the discussion here is how to bring up the children in the nurture and admonition of the Lord. *Nurture* is training by word; *admonition* is training by act and discipline, according to Trench, in his *Synonyms of the New Testament.* We must therefore use commons sense and avoid training the children in ways that deliberately make them dread the things of the Lord.

Everyone has had at least one teacher who had a pleasing disposition, knew the subject matter, and could demonstrate the practicality of it. Leaming from such a teacher is a pleasure! Should it not be so, when the father instructs his children in the ways of the Lord?

While the father instructs, the mother has law. To her falls the responsibility of most of the enforcing. That is not to absolutely separate these two; both father and mother should instruct and both should enforce. It is a matter of emphasis. The scriptural mother spends more time with the children than the father (see the discussion of 31 :10-31 in the chapter on the wife), therefore, the majority of the enforcing is at her hand. Such would require that father and mother agree on the rules as well as their penalties and rewards. Children should not be able to "play one against the other."

The "law of the mother" surely includes the "law of kindness," (31:26).

> "Hear, ye children, the instruction of a father, and attend to know understanding." (4:1)

The father's instruction should be for all the children; no favoritism should ever be shown. Each child is "the heritage of the LORD ... his reward," (Psa. 127:3). Each one is to be brought up in His nurture and admonition. Since God does not show favoritism (Rom. 2:11 and 6 other places in scripture) neither should an earthly father.

> "For I give you good doctrine, forsake ye not my law." (4:2)

Instruction should consist of doctrine. To do this, the father must listen well in church and in Bible class, as well as be diligent in his personal Bible study. He should especially emphasize those basic doctrines which are under such attack in the world: creation, inspiration and preservation of scripture, salvation by grace without works, and faithfulness to the local church. Proverbs has already emphasized separation from sinners (1:10-19), wisdom (1:20-33), and one's relationship to God (2:5 & 3:5-12). How much preparation goes into being a scriptural father! May the Lord give us fathers who have studied their Bibles and can instruct their children in doctrine!

The instruction should also include law. The word *law* emphasizes that certain things are required, and that there is a penalty for breaking that law. The father does his children a favor when he reminds them that God makes requirements, not merely suggestions, and that there are serious penalties for breaking God's laws. He has already told something of those penalties, in 1:24-32 & 2:18-22.

That father's instruction should come from experience, as the next two verses show:

> "For I was my father's son, tender and only beloved in the sight of my mother. He taught me also, and said unto me, Let thine heart retain my words: keep my commandments, and live." (4:3-4)

If the father had such a childhood, he can thank God and pass along the benefits to his children, knowing from experience the rewards of obeying the Lord. But if his father was not scriptural, he has surely learned by experience the miseries of sin, so he can warn his children strongly that they not disobey.

Parents should encourage their children to get all the wisdom they can. This theme is found often in Proverbs; see 4:7 ("Wisdom is the principal thing; therefore get wisdom: and with all thy getting get understanding.") and chapter 2, for notable examples. In our day, when Satan has almost succeeded in completely eroding our schools, both public and private, it is imperative that parents give priority to their children's getting wisdom. Not only should they be sent to the best schools, but they should also be encouraged at home to read and achieve. They should become familiar with the library as soon as they can read. They should see their parents continuing in their thirst for knowledge. Family conversation should encourage learning and whet appetites for more knowledge. God puts no premium on ignorance!

A large part of the parents' responsibility regarding the teaching of children is to guard them from the wrong kind of education. Prov. 19:27 gives this warning, "Cease, my son, to hear the instruction that causeth to err from the words of knowledge." Obviously, the "words of knowledge" are the words of God, since 1:7 has already told us that the fear of the Lord is the beginning of knowledge. We will never be able to prevent our children from hearing every error in this world, but we can faithfully teach the truth so that they will be able to recognize error, and we can believe God's promise that truth will ultimately triumph over error ("For we can do nothing against the truth, but for the truth." II Cor. 13:8).

> "The proverbs of Solomon. A wise son maketh a glad father: but a foolish son is the heaviness of his mother." (10:1)

If parents would be made glad by their children, they must seek to make them wise. Chapters 1-9 show how to do this: instruct, demonstrate, and be faithful to each other. Also, a study of the words *wise* and *foolish,* in Proverbs, will give specific details in the kind of training which produces wisdom.

The wise person:

> 1:5, hears and increases learning (see also 12:15 & 13:1)

> 10:5, gathers in summer (works without procrastination)

> 10:19, refrains his lips (controls his speech; see also 29:11)

> 11:30, wins souls

> 14:1, builds his/her house

> 14:16, fears and departs from evil

> 15:7, distributes knowledge

> 15:24, departs from hell (how important it is for parents to persuade their children to be saved!)

> 16:14, pacifies the wrath of a king

> 16:23, learns from his heart

17:10, heeds reproof more than a fool does stripes

20:26, scatters the wicked

23:23, has bought wisdom; has evidently paid the price

28:7, obeys scripture (obviously the summary and climax of it all!)

By contrast, the foolish is one who:

1:7, despises wisdom and instruction (see also 15:5)

1:22, hates knowledge

9:13, is clamorous (loud) and immoral

10:18, hates, lies, and slanders

10:23, treats mischief as a sport (modern vandalism?)

12:15, always thinks himself to be right (see also 14:3, 16; 18:2; 28:26)

12:16, is angry openly (also, 14:16-17)

13:19, thinks it is an abomination to depart from evil (also, 26:11)

14:1, plucks down his/her house

14:3, is proud (also, v. 16)

14:9, makes a mock at sin Oakes about sin, treating it lightly)

15:20, despises his/her mother

17:10, does not heed stripes (does not learn anything from punishment; see also 27:22)

17:16, has no heart for wisdom, even though he has the money for it

17:24, looks to the ends of the earth (always thinks that something else will be better, is never satisfied)

18:6, likes to argue

19:3, frets against the Lord

20:1, is deceived by wine and strong drink

20:3, meddles (interferes in other people's business)

21:20, spends, rather than saves

22:15, apparently has not had the rod of correction sufficiently applied (29:15), or correctly applied. See the chapter on the discipline of children.

29:11, tells all he knows.

Obviously, some of these characteristics of the foolish person are in all of us, naturally. We were born with the desire and ability to do several of these things. That makes us realize that the proper training will be required if these natural traits are to be overcome. That training must consist of God's word, since Psa. 19:7 promises that "the testimony of the LORD is sure, making wise the simple." The only way to turn the foolish into the wise is by the regular use of scripture, both by instruction and by example. And we can be sure that God's Word will accomplish just what He says it will.

Perhaps some parents still see foolish characteristics in their children, after they are grown. It would help us all to remember that our idea of becoming an adult at the age of eighteen years is not found in scripture. Grown men, in Bible days were still under the authority of their parents. There are many examples of their obedience; notably, the sons of Jacob when he sent them down into Egypt during the times of famine. Parents should still try to help their children, even after they are grown, if not by daily instruction, then certainly by diligent intercession. God still answers prayer! Many a parent has found that the Spirit of God can work in the heart of a thirty-year old son, etc. More will be said about this in this chapter, as we consider 22:6.

"Though hand join in hand, the wicked shall not be unpunished: but the seed of the righteous shall be delivered." (11:21) "... the house of the righteous shall stand." (12:7) "The house of the wicked shall be overthrown: but the tabernacle of the upright shall flourish." (14:11)

House often refers to the family, in scripture; compare, for example, I Tim. 3:4-5. God's promise of deliverance, security, and prosperity for the family are made to him who is righteous. The Christian has a position of righteousness, in Christ ("For he hath made him to be sin for us, who knew no sin; that we might be made the righteousness of God in him." II Cor. 5:21). But positional righteousness is only one aspect; scripture also requires practical righteousness from God's children, in such verses as I John 3:7 ("Little children, let no man deceive you: he that doeth righteousness is righteous, even as he is righteous."). The parents who would claim these promises for their family must be practicing the righteousness described in the Bible·in front of them.

The seed of the righteous shall be delivered, that is, from the miseries of sin. The house of the righteous shall stand, when God arises to judge. Contrast Mat. 7:26-27 and Psa. 15 for those who will not stand. And since the house of the wicked shall be overthrown: but the tabernacle of the upright shall flourish, it must be obvious that the actions of the parents influence the children. To understand this, we must distinguish between the penalty of sin and its· consequences.

Sin's penalty is separation from God, whether in hell, or on earth in regard to fellowship. Sin's consequences are not removed when the sin is forgiven. This is best seen by considering examples which are familiar to all: the life-long drunkard may get cirrhosis of the liver, even though he stops drinking and is converted; the gambler's family may live in poverty because of his waste and indebtedness, even though he stops gambling and gets converted; the child's emotional scars which result from being abused are not removed when the abuser gets converted.

Making this distinction between sin's penalty and its consequences helps us to understand scriptures which seem to be contradictory:

> Exe. 20:5, "Visiting the iniquity of the fathers upon the children unto the third and fourth generation of them that hate me."

> Ezk. 18:2-4, 20, "The soul that sinneth, it shall die. The son shall not bear the iniquity of the father, neither shall the father bear the iniquity of the son."

Obviously, Ezekiel was referring to the penalty of sin, while Exodus speaks of its consequences. Consider also:

> Exe. 34.7, "Keeping mercy for thousands, forgiving iniquity and transgression and sin, and that will by no means clear the guilty."

The phrase "and that will by no means clear the guilty" refers to the fact that forgiveness does not remove the consequences, a fact which is made clear in Psa. 99.8, "... Thou wast a God that forgavest them, though thou tookest vengeance on their inventions." The consequences of sin are also described in Jer. 17:2, "Whilst their children remember their altars and their groves by the green trees upon the high hills." The sin of the parents influences the children to follow suit.

Jer. 32:18 throws more light: "Thou shewest lovingkindness unto thousands, and recompensest the iniquity of the fathers into the bosom of their children after them." This last phrase shows that the sin of the fathers affected the hearts of the children ("the bosom"), either by encouraging their hearts to imitate the sin, or by discouraging their hearts to despair.

Prov. 14:11 therefore speaks of the consequences of sin. The wicked parents who waste their money on sin will see the awful results of it in their children. They could lose the house; venereal disease or AIDS could be contracted, resulting in suffering and shame. To the contrary, godliness produces the characteristics which result in honesty, hard work, compassion for the needy, and other traits which make for success.

For similar promises and warnings about the influence of parents on their children, compare 14:26; 15:25, 27; and 17:13.

> "A good man leaveth an inheritance to his children's children: and the wealth of the sinner is laid up for the just." (13:22)

It is not wrong to plan for the future, even to plan for a certain amount of financial security. For scriptural proof, see the discussion of 31:21 in the chapter on the wife.

Of course, leaving an inheritance of money must not be the priority. We are told in 15:16-17 that there is something better:

> "Better is little with the fear of the LORD than great treasure and trouble therewith. Better is a dinner of herbs where love is, than a stalled ox and hatred therewith."

If one has to choose between money and love, the choice would be obvious. However, when all the book of Proverbs is considered, the Lord promises financial blessing and earthly benefit to those who obey him.

But it would be a mistake to limit the meaning of *inheritance* to material possessions. There have been instances, in the history of God's people, when prosperity was impossible because of persecution. In such cases, the inheritance would definitely be a spiritual one. Timothy certainly inherited a great spiritual wealth from his grandmother and mother, even though his father was apparently an unbeliever; see II Tim. 1:5 and 3: 15. Without question, this spiritual inheritance of faith was worth more than any amount of material possessions.

It should go without saying that the "good man" mentioned in this verse must be a regenerated man, since Rom. 3: 12, describing the unbeliever, says that there is none that doeth good, no, not one. When God calls a person good, that one has been converted, thus having the righteousness of Christ imputed to him. Only then could the Holy One call a human being *good.*

There is probably not a more controversial subject, among believers or unbelievers, than the discipline of children. As we approach this subject, it is imperative to remember that the scripture was inspired by God; it is not the product of man's wisdom. II Pet. 1:21 clears up this matter once and for all, when it says, "For the prophecy came not in old time by the will of man: but holy men of God spake as they were moved by the Holy Ghost." Therefore, these verses are not the reasoning of Solomon in another age, which some would consider to be totally irrelevant in our day; they are the words of the eternal God, and are profitable for doctrine, reproof, correction, and for instruction in righteousness (II Tim. 3: 16).

The word *rod* seems to be the bone of contention, being variously interpreted to mean physical punishment, or verbal correction, or otherwise. A study of the Hebrew word, *shebet,* #7626 in Strong's Concordance, reveals that it may refer to:

(1) A strong weapon. It could cause death (Exo. 21 :20); it described Job's troubles (Job 9:34); it refers

to Messiah's iron rule (Psa. 2:9); it referred to Israel's oppressor (Isa. 9:4).

(2) A dart, or arrow, such as that with which Joab slew Absalom (II Sam. 18:14).

(3) A stick, used to beat out grain (Isa. 28:27).

We must conclude, therefore, that the rod refers to physical punishment. However, it certainly excludes brutality, in the case of child-discipline, for the following reasons:

(1) Prov. 23: 13-14 says, "Withhold not correction from the child: if thou beatest him with the rod, he shall not die. Thou shalt beat him with the rod and shalt deliver his soul from hell." The beating of a child with a rod, according to scriptural usage, is not harsh enough to kill him.

(2) Also, the beating with the rod is primarily for the purpose of correction, not to inflict pain. See Prov. 23:13, again.

(3) Our heavenly Father sets the chief example in the matter of chastening (see Heb. 12:6; I Cor. 10:13; and Isa. 57: 16). He is never brutal. He does not inflict pain for that purpose, but rather to produce holiness. And it is never more than a person can bear!

A little common sense would show that scripture never condones, or even suggests, child brutality. If God put his approval on the fact that "a righteous man regardeth the life of his beast," (12: 10), He surely would not encourage being brutal to a child. Solomon has already told us that he was "tender and only beloved in the sight of (his) mother," (4:3); it would be unthinkable, even from a mere human standpoint, for such a person to advocate violence upon children.

Beside all that, our verse under consideration says, "he that *loveth* him chasteneth him betimes." No one can lovingly brutalize a child!

Therefore, there is no ground for the enemies of scripture to accuse the Bible of teaching child brutality. And there is certainly no biblical basis for any twisted mind to use God's Word as a basis for molesting children.

The rod refers to physical punishment, which is administered lovingly. And it is administered *betimes,* which means *early.* The Hebrew word is so translated in 1:28 and 8:17. This means early in life, because the scriptures teach that we are born sinners (Psa. 58:3 and Isa. 48:8), but it should not be before the child understands, since 29:15 says that the rod gives wisdom. If the child is unable to understand what is happening and cannot get wisdom from the situation, it is too early to use the rod. It is not enough for them to react out of fear; an animal can do that. The child must be able to have at least an elementary understanding of something being wrong and causing suffering. This ability of children is mentioned in Isa. 7:16. Any parent who wants wisdom from the Lord in order to recognize when the proper time for chastening has come can claim James 1:5 and get it.

Betimes also means early after the offence. Children forget quickly. Too many times a parent has waited "until we get home" and the little one has forgotten. In such a case, no wisdom is imparted; there is only hurt and misunderstanding. Of course, parents must be wise and not choose public, unfriendly places to discipline their children, unless they want to go to jail! In our day of so much child brutality, many people have over-reacted to every form of physical punishment and have had innocent people arrested. A place of privacy is much better, not only for that reason, but also so that proper instruction can be given the child while it is not distracted by being humiliated before an audience.

Why are we so lax in physical chastening? Charles Bridges said it this way: "The indulgence of our children has its roots in self-indulgence ... we do not like putting ourselves to pain." The remedy is to consider what God says the end result of not chastening will be; then seek God's help in administering the rod in a loving manner.

> "Children's children are the crown of old men; and
> the glory of children are their fathers." (17:6).

It is implied here that the "old men" are righteous; we have already learned in 10:27 that "the fear of the Lord prolongeth days, but the years of the wicked shall be shortened." We therefore assume that the old men are old because they feared the Lord and He prolonged their days. As a contrast, how many families have been broken because of sin, so that parents· did not know where children went and never saw their grandchildren!

Fathers who are the glory of their children will enjoy their grandchildren. The children will naturally want their offspring to glory in the same man. Respect is contagious.

> "He that begetteth a fool doeth it to his sorrow: and
> the father of a fool hath no joy." (17:21)

Are fools begotten? No doubt, the sin nature is in view. The implication here is that this father has made no effort to counteiact this innate propensity. For the description of the fool, see notes on 10: I, in this chapter.

> "House and riches are the inheritance of
> fathers: and a prudent wife is from the LORD." (19:14)

As we have done so many times, we must see that obedience to previous instruction is implied. Prov. 15 gave us the principle; the wisdom in this book is progressive. "A wise man will hear, and will increase learning." It is unwise to jump into the middle of the book and try to apply any verse to any person! The *riches* which are promised by the Lord to a father are evidently the right kind of riches, that is, those which have been obtained from:

3:9-10, tithing

8:18, wisdom (see also 24:3-4)

10:2, righteousness

10:22, God's blessing

11:1, honesty (also 21:6)

11:16, saving

13:11 & 14:23, labor

but not from greed, 15:27. Later, more will be learned about the right way to obtain riches. In 19:17, by charity; in 20:21 & 28:20, 22, by patience; in 22:4, by humility and the fear of the Lord.

Riches which are obtained in a scriptural manner should be the inheritance of fathers; godly children and grand-children should enjoy the benefits of God's blessing.

The last half of the verse was discussed in the chapter on the husband.

> "Chasten thy son while there is hope, and let not thy soul spare for his crying." (19:18)

The implication is that there is coming a time when there will be no hope. It may be when there is no more opportunity to chasten; therefore, do it early, as we were admonished in 13:24. We must not lessen the instruction because it is painful. The priority is not pleasure, but correction.

Chastening must always be with a view to correction, not because the chastener wants to inflict pain, or has been embarrassed. Scriptural chastening is accomplished by three means:

(1) punishment (Lev. 26:18, 23, 28)

(2) scripture (Deut. 4:36 & Isa. 8:11)

(3) words (Prov. 13:1)

Too often we omit the scripture! Of course, it must be done in such a way that the child will not hate scripture. It might be wise to wait until the suffering is over, when the "loving period" comes, to refer to scripture as the reason for chastening and to give the moral lesson.

The evidence that a man is just is two-fold: his walk of integrity, and the blessing which is upon his children. God's Word is always practical; it is not what a person claims, but what he shows, that tells people what kind of person he is.

We note that his walk is not determined by circumstances but by integrity. A good example is David, when he had so many opportunities to kill Saul and assume the throne for which he had already been anointed. He repeatedly refused to slay Saul because he would not touch God's anointed. His belief that God would remove Saul and elevate him to the throne constituted his integrity and dictated his actions. Thus he proved himself to be a just man, and was known to be so, especially by Saul, Saul's soldiers and David's men.

Another excellent example is Joseph, who refused to commit adultery with Potiphar's wife. She saw his integrity first hand; so did the Lord! Even though no one else did, at that time, God thought enough of it to record it in His eternal Word.

Hannah is an outstanding illustration of a just woman. Because of her integrity, she gave her only son, Samuel, to the Lord, just as she had promised to do when she originally asked for the child. This request was a silent one (see I Sam. 1:11-13); only God heard it. If Hannah had been concerned only with her reputation among people, she would have conveniently forgotten that commitment. Also, if she had been selfish, she certainly would have kept her only son for her own enjoyment, and as living proof that she had silenced her adversary, Peninah. Instead of all this, she showed that she was just and was a woman of integrity; she kept her vow to God and presented Samuel at the tabernacle, as soon as he was weaned. As a result, her son was certainly blessed after her.

The children are blessed because they have a godly example to follow. Integrity makes one keep his promises to God; it also makes a person be honest in relationships with people; it generates the desire to do quality work, to save, to spend wisely, and to do a host of other things that will be imitated by the children who observe them.

Here is another verse in Proverbs which teaches that people do what they do because they are what they are!

> "Train up a child in the way he should go: and when he is old, he will not depart from it." (Prov. 22:6)

This tremendous admonition and promise is for parents, prospective parents, grandparents, relatives, and anyone else who has a heart for children! It is absolutely reliable, since "all the promises of God in him are yea, and in him Amen, unto the glory of God by us," (II Cor. 1:20). The true and living God, who cannot lie, will keep this promise; our responsibility lies in the first word, *train*. But before we get to that, we must consider *the way*.

Some interpreters understand this to mean "his way," that is, the child's way. They say that parents and teachers must learn the natural inclinations of the child and direct him thus. To prove that this is the wrong explanation, we need only consider Isa. 53:6, "All we like sheep have gone astray; we have turned every one to his own way; and the

LORD hath laid on him the iniquity of us all."

Since the verse says, "All we," that must include children. Every child has already turned "to his own way;" he does not need to be trained in it. Worst of all, the Lord describes "turning to our own way" as "the iniquity of us all," and reveals the outrage of that iniquity by telling us that it was what Christ bore on the cross. Clearly, then, we do not need to train up a child in his own way, which is sin, in God's sight.

Charles Bridges said that when a child is born, two ways lie before it: the way in which he would go, and the way in which he should go. That says it succinctly!

Psa. 58:3 teaches us that the child begins going his own way, which is iniquity, immediately after birth. "The wicked are estranged from the womb; they go astray *as soon as they be born*, speaking lies." How often does the scripture teach that we are born sinners! All the more reason for training the child in the way that he *should* go.

The way is God's way. A parallel verse, Gen. 18:19, shows this; note the emphasized phrase: "For I know him, that he will command his children and his household after him, and they shall keep *the way of the LORD*, to do justice and judgment; that the LORD may bring upon Abraham that which he hath spoken of him." God knew that Abraham's children would keep, not their own way, nor some counselor's way, nor the world's way, but the way of the Lord.

The significance of this phrase will be seen when we consider the fact that many people do not believe Prov. 22:6, because they have seen some child who was brought up in a Christian home turn out to be less than perfect. We seem to think that Prov. 22:6 is a promise of sinless perfection, so that if a child does anything wrong, either the verse is not true, or the child's training was not scriptural. That mistake will be recognized and forsaken when we realize that "the way he should go" is the Lord's way, but it does not mean sinless perfection. How can we be sure? By remembering that God said that Abraham's children would keep His way; then by reading about the lives and doings of Isaac and Ishmael. They certainly were not perfect!

Thus by comparing scripture with scripture, we have learned, so far, that "the way he should go" is not his own way (Isa. 53:6), but the Lord's way (Gen. 18: 19), and that keeping God's way does not mean sinless perfection. What, then, does "keeping the Lord's way" mean? It describes the worship of the true and living God. Both Isaac and Ishmael did some things wrong (see Gen. 16:12 & 26:7), but they never went after a false god.

Another good example is David. Even though scripture records several of his sins (see 1 Sam 27:8-12 for example), God describes his whole life in I Kings 15:5 by saying, "David did that which was right in the eyes of the LORD, and turned not aside from any thing that he commanded him all the days of his life, save only in the matter of Uriah the Hittite." Since "all scripture is inspired of God," (II Tim. 3: 16) this must be a true description. There will be no problem if we remember that, when God speaks of someone who has kept His way, or who has done right in His eyes, he is speaking of the worship of the true God as opposed to idols. David never turned aside from worshipping God and His commands regarding such.

To prove that "keeping God's way" means worshipping Him as opposed to worshipping idols, we need only consider the description of Amon, in II Kings 21 :21-22. "And he walked in all the way that his father walked in, and served the idols that his father served, and worshipped them: And he forsook the LORD God of his fathers, and walked not in the way of the LORD." Clearly, "walking not in the way of the LORD" was equal to "serving idols."

For an opposite example, let's consider II Kings 22:2, describing Josiah; "And he did that which was right in the sight of the LORD, and walked in all the way of David his father, and turned not aside to the right hand or to the left."

Another mistake which is often made regarding the promise in Prov. 22:6 is thinking that someone is either 100% successful, regarding the training of his children, or 100% a failure. We have already seen that God does not look at it that way, when we considered Isaac, Ishmael, and David. A little common sense and observation will teach us that parents may succeed in training their children to believe the right doctrine, but fail in teaching them to pray every day. Likewise, some parents succeed in training their children to be faithful to church, but they fail to teach them to be soulwinners. There are degrees of success and failure. Real life shows us that there are faithful church members, even church leaders, who are not holy. And, some are more holy than others. These are good examples of the fact that there are degrees of success and failure.

Parents are responsible to train their children in all that is included in "the way of the Lord." That one way would include many ways. We often forget that, assuming that one or two things are all that is important. We must not only train them to be saved, but also to be spiritual. Training is necessary if they are to know the Bible, if they are to get answers to their prayers, if they are to be soulwinners.

If parents fail to train their children in some particular way, they will be letting the world do the training. If we fail to teach our children to live holy lives, we will be letting Holly$_{yw}$ood train them to be unholy. There is no way to prevent their exposure to Holly$_{yw}$ood. Even if there is no television, no movie-going, no rock music, children will learn about those things by simply being in this world. The influence of Holl$_{y\,w}$ ood is pervasive; no part of life escapes it. How much more, therefore, should godly parents train their children in matters of holiness, to offset the evil influence which they will naturally receive.

If we fail to teach them the misery of drinking wine, Hollywood will convince them that wine is a necessary part of a tasty meal, especially if it is to be romantic. Unless we teach them biblical morality, Hollywood will convince them that adultery and various other forms of immorality are the normal way of life.

Even though we cannot prevent their exposure to these evils, we can certainly counteract them with the power of scripture! And that is where the word *train* comes in.

Why did the Lord say, "Train?" Why not, "Lecture?" In all sports, there is a trainer. It is not training when the athletic director lectures the players that they should go out and become stars. It is training when a person who already knows what to do shows others how do it; then, when the player does something wrong, the trainer corrects him and shows him how to do it properly. In most cases, the player must practice the particular play several times before he becomes proficient at it. In other words, it is a process of teaching, showing, correcting, practicing, and repetition. Usually, there is a lot of trial and error. There probably has never been an athlete who did everything perfectly; all make mistakes. The trainer does not give up after one or two mistakes. The player· is not kicked off the team for one or two mistakes. The trainer is not considered a failure when a player makes a mistake. We should think of these things when we consider the Lord's admonition that we should "train up a child in the way he should go."

When should we begin? Hannah gives us a good example, in I Sam. 1:24, "And when she had weaned him, she took him up with her, with three bullocks, and one ephah of flour, and a bottle of wine, and brought him unto the house of the Lord in Shiloh: and the child was young." Some commentators say that the Jews, at that time, did not wean their children until the age of two or three years. That may seem like a long time to us, with our modem ways, but it might have been, especially when we consider that milk would not have been as available to them as it is to us. Even if that explanation be accurate, Samuel was still very young to be surrendered by his mother to live in the house of the Lord!

Samuel was born in the priestly line; but according to scripture, the priest did not assume priestly duties until the age of thirty. If Hannah had been like many mothers, she would have forgotten all about religious training until just before Samuel turned thirty! To the contrary, she began early; she "lent him to the Lord" at the age of two or three, to begin learning the ways of serving God as His priest. Waiting until thirty could be too late; Samuel could have been set in the ways of wickedness and have no interest in the things of God. Hannah was wise; let us imitate her godly example.

We must not consider working in the nursery and other children's classes to be a glorified baby-sitting job, but a scriptural opportunity to train the little ones in the ways of Christ. We must not consider mothers who give their lives to the training of their young children to be unintelligent, or incapable of having a "career" in this world, as so many think today. Training young children is scriptural, challenging, and extremely wise! It does require much thinking, praying, and preparation; perhaps that is why so many look for ways to avoid it. But there is not a greater challenge than that of teaching biblical truth to little ones. If a person cannot put the truth of the gospel on the level of a child, that person does not understand the gospel very well.

Every Christian parent would like for his/her child to turn out like Samuel; if that occurs, we must do as Hannah did and being early.

If we begin early, we must repeat the training, according to Prov. 22:6, until the child is *old*. But when is one old, in biblical language? In many cases today, people think that, after children become teenagers, you cannot do anything with them. Yet ask a twenty-one-year-old man if he considers himself to be old and see what he says. Ask a thirty-year-old woman if she is old! Both common sense and scripture teach us that *old* does not mean the teen-age years.

Gen. 42 & 43 give us examples of Jacob's commanding his sons to go to Egypt to get food. Egypt was several hundred miles away and that trip would have to be made by walking, or riding some animal, or in some uncomfortable wagon. Every one of those sons was married and had children, yet Jacob did not hesitate to command them to make such an arduous journey; and, as far as the scriptural record is concerned, there was no resistance on the part of any son to that command. Jacob did not believe, as many do today, that you cannot do anything with them when they get grown. Of course, people today object to this reasoning by saying that these events occurred in another time when customs were different. While we admit that this is true, we should remind ourselves that God gave us details such as these in His Word for "doctrine, reproof, correction, and instruction in righteousness," (II Tim. 3: 16). We will not find a better example than those given in the Bible.

Hannah continued her concern for Samuel; I Sam. 2: 19 says that she brought him a coat from year to year, when she came up with her husband to offer the yearly sacrifice.

Another proof of the fact that God holds parents responsible to keep training their children, even after they are grown, is found in I Sam. 2 & 3. In 2:22, we learn of the sin of Eli's sons: "Now Eli was very old, and heard all that his sons did unto all Israel; and how they lay with the women that assembled at the door of the tabernacle of the congregation." It is obvious that these sons were grown men. We learn later that they were married. God tells us, in 3: 13, that Eli was both responsible and negligent regarding the actions of his sons: "For I have told him that I will judge his house for ever for the iniquity which he knoweth; because his sons made themselves vile, and he restrained them not." Eli's responsibility was so great, in the eyes of God, that he pronounced judgment on his house because Eli made no effort to restrain them. We must carefully note that, it was not Eli's fault that they sinned, but rather that he restrained them not. Did he say, as so many do today, that nothing could be done with them after they were grown? God showed him to be wrong!

The fact is that all young people rebel against righteousness; some to a greater degree, some not so much. Solomon is a good example; he was taught by his father and mother, according to Prov. 4:1-5 and chapter 31, but he rebelled in many ways. When he repented, he wrote Ecclesiastes to record his confession and repentance. He was speaking from experience, when he wrote the words of Eccl. 11:9-10, "Rejoice, 0 young man, in thy youth; and let thy heart cheer thee in the days of thy youth, and walk in the ways of thine heart, and in the sight of thine eyes; but know thou, that for all these things God will bring thee into judgment. Therefore remove sorrow from thy heart, and put away evil from thy flesh: for childhood and youth are vanity."

He knew that young people like to be happy ("let thy heart cheer thee"), that they like to do whatever they desire ("walk in the ways of thine heart"), and that they like to do what they see immediately, not caring about the unseen future ("and in the sight of thine eyes"). Because this is true of all young people, they will do wrong. The desire of their heart is sin, according to Jer. 17:9, "The heart is deceitful above all things, and desperately wicked." This describes the heart of every single person who has ever been born, except Christ, because of Psa. 33: 15, "He fashioneth their hearts alike." We are all alike, in the evil of our hearts. That evil does not always express itself in the same way, but the basic evil is there. All young people sin, no matter how good their training.

When the young man walks "in the ways of his heart and in the sight of (his) eyes" he is sinning, because the verse ends by saying, "for all these things God will bring thee into judgment." Every young person rebels! Some do it outwardly and brazenly; others keep it inside. When the rebellion shows itself, many parents think they are failures, or that the Bible verse is not true, or is not for our dispensation, or that scriptural training did no good, or some other such depressing reaction. To the contrary, when we see the rebellion, or learn later that it existed in the heart, we should realize that this simply *proves* the Bible!

Another proof of this is found in Heb. 12:2, where Christ is called "the author and finisher of our faith." Most of us realize that we cannot be the author of anyone's faith; we cannot make people believe. We give the Word, but God does the work which results in believing (see John 6:29). We also need to realize that we can no more be the finisher, than we could be the author! Our witness, our example, and our training are necessary, but we do not finish anyone's faith. That is the work of Christ, and He continues to work all through that believer's life to accomplish it.

Solomon was trained right, but rebelled in his youth. Then, when he was old, he did exactly what Prov. 22:6 promises: he did not depart from the training of his early days. Another example is Manasseh, the son of godly King Hezekiah.

Hezekiah was certainly not perfect, but he was a praying man (read Isa. 37 & 38), along with being humble (II Chron. 32:26). Most of us would like to get answers to our prayers in the spectacular way that he did! He must have trained Manasseh correctly, besides giving him some good examples to follow, because we read that even though Manasseh committed some awful sins when he was young (II Chron. 33: 1-10), he did repent when we was old. Verses 11-19 give us these thrilling words: "And when he was in affliction, he besought the LORD his God, and humbled himself greatly before the God of his fathers, and prayed unto him: and he was entreated of him, and heard his supplication, and brought him again to Jerusalem into his kingdom. Then Manasseh knew that the LORD he was God . . . and he took away the strange gods . . . and he repaired the altar of the LORD ... His prayer also, and how God was entreated of him . . . behold, they are written among the sayings of the seers."

In the light of all these scriptures, let us realize that the heart of every young person has the seed of rebellion in it. The training which is spoken of in Prov. 22:6 is required repeatedly, until he is old. It is when he is old that he will not depart from it, and *old* does not mean sixteen, or twenty -five.

This training must not only be repetitious, but it must be with scripture. Lois and Eunice, Timothy's grandmother and mother, are good examples. II Tim. 3:15 says, of

Timothy, "From a child thou hast known the holy scriptures, which are able to make thee wise unto salvation through faith which is in Christ Jesus."

We should teach children the doctrines of scripture, helping them to memorize key verses where these doctrines are found, as well as verses which promise victory and encourage faith. Children can memorize easily, much more so than adults; therefore, let us teach them to memorize the Bible in their early years. John Newton was converted as an adult, after many years of sin, directly because of the scripture which his mother had taught him to memorize before he was seven years old!

Some parents try this briefly, then stop because they do not see immediate results. Again, scripture will correct this error. Lois and Eunice taught Timothy, but he was not saved until he was a teenager and that was through the preaching of Paul (see I Tim. 1:2 and I Cor. 4:15). God's Word always has its promised results, although they may not come immediately, or in the way that we anticipated. Are we willing for someone else to win our children to Christ, to reap where we have sowed? Sometimes that is God's way (John 4:37-38), and we certainly cannot improve on it. Faithfulness to obey the Lord always brings the fulfillment of His promise in His time and His way. It takes parents and preachers and teachers and witnesses. Paul had no children, but he reached the children of others.

Taking the children to church is not enough. It is vital, but it is not all that God requires. We must teach them the scripture, a responsibility which is found not only in the New Testament, but also in the Old. Psa. 78 gives us good instruction:

(1) We should teach our children what our parents taught us. Vs. 3, "... which we have heard and known, and our fathers have told us."

(2) In teaching children Bible stories, we should emphasize the power of God. Vs. 4, "We will not hide them from their children, shewing to the generation to come the praises of the LORD, and his strength, and his wonderful works that he hath done." When we tell about David and Goliath, let us not only mention David's courage, but the power of God in giving that great victory. How often is the credit given to David, or to luck! Likewise, Samson's great strength was not due to his long hair, but to his obedience to God and God's resulting power.

(3) We should tell the children that one of the purposes for which God gave the Bible is that we might teach it to the little ones. Vs. 5, "For he established a testimony in Jacob, and appointed a law in Israel, which he commanded our fathers, that they should make them known to their children." God wants the little ones to know that the Bible is for them.

(4) They should learn it so that they can teach it to their children. Vs. 6, "That the generation to come might know them, even the children which should be born, who should arise and declare them to their children."

(5) We should teach the children to set their hope in God and not repeat the sins of their ancestors. Vs. 7-8, "That they might set their hope in God, and not forget the works of God, but keep his commandments: and might not be as their fathers, a stubborn and rebellious generation."

Thus we are to teach children the scriptures *and* the reasons for learning them.

In doing all this, the proper attitude is vital. Children can see through the hypocrisy of adults easily. They learn to know what we are like before they can even understand our words; they read our facial expressions, they notice our actions, they see our priorities. They learn to discern people before they learn language! When they learn to speak, then to read and write, they do not lose that ability. They still notice the tone of voice and the facial expressions of others; it is a result of several years' experience. Even when they are teenagers, they can spot a h_{yp}ocritical adult almost immediately. Anyone who has worked with them knows this well. Therefore, we must have the proper attitude. Christ emphasized this in his ·stinging condemnation of the Pharisees and scribes:

"Well hath Esaias prophesied of you hypocrites, as it is written, This people honoureth me with their lips, but their heart is far from me." (Mark 7:6). What was the end result of such hypocrisy? Vs. 13, "Making the word of God of none effect through your tradition," (which was an outgrowth of their evil hearts). If we are not genuine in our obedience to the Lord, our teaching of the children, taking them to church, etc. will nullify scripture.

If we teach our children to pray, they must see us praying. If we teach them that the Bible is God's Word, they must see us reading it and loving it. If we insist that they go to church, we must go with them and always speak constructively about the house of the Lord before them. If we teach them about hell and heaven, they must be urged to repent and believe on Christ for the salvation of their souls. If we see them misbehave in church, we must be sure that our correction is from a motive of wanting them to do right, rather than from being embarrassed before others. If they hear us praise the Lord in church, they ought to hear us praise the Lord in the business world, and in the hospital, and at the cemetery.

Titus 2:7 emphasizes this very responsibility, by saying, "In all things shewing thyself a pattern of good works. .. sincerity ... sound speech that cannot be condemned." Who would receive even the choicest food from a leprous hand? The condition of the one who gives the word is important. The prodigal son assumed that his father would receive him; had he seen that attitude before? No doubt the father had shown forgiveness many times in that young man's life, perhaps toward him, perhaps toward others, so much so that he did not even entertain the possibility that he would be rejected. That speaks volumes for the father's example!

Almost everything we learn is from an example. How long would it take for a child to learn to tie shoe laces, if he only heard a lecture on it? Children learn to pray from hearing others pray. Parents ought to take their children with them when they try to win lost souls. They will learn to witness and win by seeing it done. They will learn daily Bible reading by being a part of that as they grow up. They will learn to pay attention and get something from a sermon if they see parents doing it, then hear them discussing the message later. They learn tithing when they see the years of blessing on their parents who have thus obeyed the Lord.

All of these suggestions and directions will be energized by prayer. Without prayer, they will probably have little effect. A good example is Manoah, the father of Samson, in Judges 13: 12. After the angel had revealed to his wife that they would have a son, who would be the deliverer of Israel, he prayed for directions in training that child. "And Manoah said, Now let thy words come to pass. How shall we order the child, and how shall we do unto him?" We note that the angel did not merely say, "Use the Bible," but gave him specific directions to be followed. The vow of a Nazarite was not for everyone, although it was a part of scripture.

We must pray about each child. There are scriptures which all should obey; there are others for specific ones. We may not know what the future holds for each of our children, but the Lord does. If we seek Him, He will direct us to those portions which are needed by each one. God knows whom

He will call to preach, or to teach, or to be a deacon; He knows who will be a father or mother; He has plans for some to be leaders and some to be followers. Beside that, each child is an individual, not only in his personality, but in his particular needs and problems and temptations to sin. Why are some people slaves to alcohol, while others may drink "moderately" and never get drunk? Why are some slaves to gambling, while others may take it or leave it? We do not have the answers, but we know that God has perfect knowledge of each child and can direct the praying parent and teacher to the specific verses which would meet that child's need.

How many mothers have known that a newborn boy would be a preacher? We have heard such testimony. Is it not likely that she would have taught that boy all along, with that in mind? What if the Lord revealed that a boy or girl would be a missionary. Would not those parents do their utmost to keep that child from having any racial prejudice?

Sunday school teachers should also pray for the children, individually. It is also helpful to visit in the homes, trying to know them a little better, so that specific teaching may be given. We know very little about people when we see them only church. Our prayers are limited. This is a good lesson for preachers, also!

After all this, a parent or teacher may be overwhelmed. This may seem like an impossible task. Also, one may be conscious of failure and be quite depressed. Sometimes, we think we are doing very well, then, without warning, everything caves in, sin is committed, and we think that we completely failed. But, we must remember that we will all fail, to some extent. What then shall we do?

The Holy Spirit inspired the book of Ecclesiastes to show us exactly what to do in such a situation. If there was ever a failure, it was Solomon! He rebelled against all his training and even disobeyed divine revelation, but one thing can be said in his favor: he did confess that failure and repent of it, then he showed it by exhorting others not to follow his example.

In Ecc. 7:26-28, he confessed that he had disobeyed God by marrying seven hundred wives and three hundred concubines (see Deut. 17: 17). He confessed that he was a sinner when he was taken in by them. His sinful attitude made him look for the wrong kind in the first place, and he found them. Then, in 9:9, he corrected that, exhorting others to "Live joyfully with the wife whom thou lovest all the days of the life of thy vanity, which he hath given thee ... " We note that he did not say "the wives," but "the wife." And he emphasized that it should be the wife "whom he hath given thee." Here, then, was a preacher who went wrong, but has repented; now he is instructing his children not to follow his example, but to do right in God's eyes. He has explained to them the misery and heartache of sin. He has not tried to cover up, or make excuse. Such is true confession and repentance.

More evidence is found in 12:9-14. Instead of brooding about his backslidings and failures, he not only confessed and repented, but made a sincere effort to warn others. "And moreover, because the preacher was wise (remember that God had given him this wisdom, and that God's gifts are without repentance, Rom. 11 :29), he still taught the people knowledge; yea, he gave good heed, and sought out, and set in order many proverbs (this required a lot of work. Are we willing to work that hard in teaching our children?)."

He tried to get just the verses that each child needed (vs. 10, "The preacher sought to find out acceptable words."). He taught them that God's word will motivate us (vs. 11, "The words of the wise are as goads"), so that they would seek the scripture when they are discouraged, or backslidden. He emphasized that the Bible would give them stability ("and as nails fastened by the masters of assemblies"). He stressed that the Bible, even though written by many men, actually all came from one true God ("which are given from one shepherd"). The Lord, who is our shepherd, has given us His words, which will do everything for us that we need. How necessary it is that the child learn who the author of the Bible is: He is the good shepherd, who gave His life for the sheep. A shepherd never leaves his sheep; children need to learn that, if they know the Lord Jesus Christ as personal Saviour, they will never be alone!

People drink alcohol because they are lonely; they take drugs for the same reason. Likewise, people sell their bodies; others commit suicide, all because they are lonely. Knowing Christ, the good shepherd, would prevent all that. He said, "I will never leave thee, nor forsake thee. So that we may boldly say, The Lord is my helper, and I will not fear what man shall do unto me." (Heb. 13:5-6).

May the Lord help us to believe Prov. 22:6 and obey it, sincerely expecting the promised results.

> "Foolishness is bound in the heart of a child; but the rod of correction shall drive it far from him." (22:15)

All children inherited the sin nature from their parents, even if they were godly. Psa. 58:3 proves this, when it says, "The wicked are estranged from the womb; they go astray as soon as they be born, speaking lies." (cf. 51:5) The fact that this verse describes everyone is shown by Isa. 53:6, "All we like sheep have gone astray, we have turned every one to his own way, and the LORD hath laid on him the iniquity of us all." The *foolishness* is naturally there; it does not have to be learned. Every parent who has observed his children knows this. But what does scripture mean by the word *foolishness?* The Hebrew word is translated *folly, foolishly,* and *foolishness.*

Here is a summary:

> Prov. 5:23, it causes one to go astray.

> Prov. 13:16, it is obvious.

> Prov. 14:8, it is deceit. This shows that the word as used in scripture is much more serious than the way we use it today. *Foolishness* is lying.

> Prov. 14:29, it is shown by haste of spirit (we would say, "loss of temper"). Compare 14:17.

> Prov. 15:21, it is enjoyed by him who is destitute of wisdom.

> Prov. 17:12, it is more dangerous than a bear robbed of her whelps.

> Prov. 18: 13, it is shown by hasty, uninformed answers.

> Prov. 19:3, it causes a perverted way and rebellion against the Lord.

> Prov. 27:22, it will not be purged by physical punishment, alone!

> Psa. 38:5, it is equal to sin. Compare Psa. 69.5 and Prov. 24.9.

Thus we see *that foolishness* in scriptural language is sin. It is naturally in the child.

When we are told that the rod of correction shall drive it far from him, we must remember that the rod of correction is not merely physical punishment. This is proved by 27:22, "Though thou shouldest bray a fool in a mortar among wheat with a pestle, yet will not his foolishness depart from him." So, mere physical pain will not cure foolishness. The foolish child must not only be disciplined physically, but also corrected from scripture and shown a godly example, as we have already seen in the discussion of 22:6.

Foolishness is bound in the *heart*, which includes the desires (6.25), the emotions (15:13, 15), and the thoughts (23:7). Correction must therefore be applied to the particular area where foolishness is detected. We must not use the rod merely to inflict punishment; neither should we use scripture to berate the foolish child. We must search the scripture for the appropriate verses which may be judiciously applied to the particular need in the child. Does he have foolish thoughts? Isa. 26:3 would be good to use. The spiritual parent will be ever searching the scripture for appropriate verses to use in training children. We must think ahead, anticipating the problems which will be evident in the child. It is good to make notes of scripture which would correct wrong desires, wrong emotions, and wrong thoughts. A Bible student might begin by using the blank pages at the beginning and end of his Bible. How much better this would be than to simply collect signatures on those pages!

This rod of correction will have to be applied repeatedly; see the discussion of 22: 6, under the word *train*.

> "The father of the righteous shall greatly rejoice: and he that begetteth a wise child shall have joy of him." (23:24)

This promise is the opposite of that found in 10: 1. See the notes on that verse for the meaning of *wise*.

> "Through wisdom is an house builded; and by understanding it is established: and by knowledge shall the chambers be filled with all precious and pleasant riches." (24:3-4)

Several comparisons may be made between the house and the family: (1) The house is built by wisdom; to build a family, one must know how to begin and how to succeed. Thus we have all these instructions in Proverbs. (2) The house is established by understanding, that is, a house is secure when one knows how to protect it from the elements, etc.; the family will be filled with both necessities and luxuries by knowing what Proverbs teaches about the proper way to get them. See the notes on 19:14, for God's promise and instructions.

We should pray that our children might be filled with the knowledge of God's will in all wisdom and spiritual understanding, just as Paul did for the Colossians, in Col. 1:9. The same three words are found in the first six verses of Proverbs; thus we may get them from a careful study and application of this book. They will not be obtained by the lazy; Prov. 2: 1-9 and 18: 1 show that much effort is required.

Prov. 4: 1 teaches that understanding may be learned from parents. Then, 5: 1 and following verses emphasize that all three words have to do with moral purity. They must be sought daily, according to 8:34. They have their beginning in the fear of the Lord and in the knowledge of His holiness (9: 10 & 28:5). Winning souls is an evidence of wisdom (11 :30). An evidence of knowledge is not talking so much (17:27)!

All these facts, learned from Proverbs, give the parents much material to use in preparing their children to build a house and a family.

This has been a lengthy chapter, and may seem to be impossible to obey. However, we should remember that these things may be learned by repeated practice, through the years. God's commands are not grievous (I John 5:3), that is, they are not hard to bear, not severe, not deplorable. They can be obeyed by the born-again Christian. When we fail, we should confess it and receive forgiveness, then try again! "A just man falleth seven times, and riseth up again," (24: 16). In the mercy of God, He has not given us only one chance to obey, but a whole lifetime. If we keep trying and trusting Him, we will surely receive the promised benefits.

Chapter 4

The Child's Responsibility

As we noted in the introduction, many verses of Proverbs are addressed to one or more children. Children are often told to obey their parents in this world, but here in Proverbs, they are told exactly how to do it!

> "My son, hear the instruction of thy father, and forsake not the law of thy mother: For they shall be an ornament of grace unto thy head, and chains about thy neck." (1:8-9)

Children are to obey both parents, "thy father . . . thy mother." There should be no "playing of the one against the other." We should not try to get one parent to change what the other has said.

When scripture says *hear,* it means to obey. For instance, Rom. 10:17 tells us, "Faith cometh by hearing, and hearing by the word of God." Obviously, not every person who hears a Bible verse being read receives faith from it; it is only those who do what scripture says, who experience faith being created in their hearts. In the same way, Christ rebuked the Pharisees because they did not hear His words (see John 8:47). How could He say that, when they were standing right there, listening to Him? He obviously meant that they were not obeying God's word.

By comparing the word *hear* with other words and phrases in these opening passages of Proverbs, we learn that it also means:

Forsake not (1:8)

Obey (1:10, 15)

Receive (2:1-4)

Remember (3:1)

This last one, remember, is probably the hardest! How can we improve our memory? Once again, Proverbs helps us. We remember by:

> Keeping, 3:1 (that is, obeying. We remember those things which we do the most often)
>
> Review, 6:21 ("Bind them continually upon thine heart")
>
> Do it publicly, 6:21 ("Tie them about thy neck")
>
> Live by the commands, 7:3 ("Bind them upon thy fingers")

The child is *never* to forsake his mother's law. The Lord Jesus still felt responsible for his mother's welfare, even when He was on the cross! See John 19:26-27, where He made provision for John to take care of her. Another example is the Rechabites, Jer. 35:8-10, 18-19. Even after they were grown men, they obeyed what their father had taught them and God rewarded them accordingly. Of course, this would exclude sin; God nowhere commands a child to continue obeying parents after he is grown, when they want you to sin. Christ showed that clearly, in Mat. 10:35-37, where He said that some would have to forsake father and mother because of Him. That does not mean to forsake supporting them, but to forsake their will if it conflicts with God's will. Read those verses, before you jump to any conclusions!

God promises that the child's obedience will be "an ornament of grace unto thy head, and chains about thy neck," that is, it will be beautiful. And this beauty ought to be preferred over the worldly kind. After all, common sense teaches us that not very many people are beautiful, physically, and us that not many can afford the beauty that comes with beautiful possessions, but every single person can be beautiful spiritually, and should be. A similar passage is I Pet. 3:3-4, emphasizing spiritual attractiveness over the physical.

This admonition is so important that it is repeated in 6:20-21. Then, verse 22 gives the results of such obedience: proper direction of life (preventing immorality, vv. 24-35), security, and companionship. These are things that everyone says they want; they are promised by the God who cannot lie, to the child who obeys both parents.

Likewise, God makes promises to those who are wise. For instance, wouldn't it be great to understand "the fear of the Lord?" So many people do not know what that means; even Bible scholars disagree in their definitions. But a certain kind of person can definitely understand it. That same person will understand righteousness, and judgment, and equity, and every good path, according to 2:5 & 9. What do we have to do to get such understanding?

> "My son, if thou wilt receive my words, and hide my commandments with thee . . ." (2:1)

It is necessary to take in the words of a godly parent, and memorize them. Something else is required:

> "So that thou incline thine ear unto wisdom . . ." (v. 2a)

Inclining the ear toward something requires leaning away from something! A deliberate decision has to be made not to listen to the things of the world, if we are to hear the things of God from a godly parent. Many passages in Proverbs warn us away from immorality, dishonesty, and laziness. We have to turn away from anything that would encourage these, and that would include any music, magazines, television, movies, books, and companions which promote them. Everyone knows that these are being done, so there is no need for proof. The need is for a conscious decision to turn away from them, so that orte can "incline the ear unto wisdom."

> " . . . and apply thine heart to understanding . . ."(vs. 2b)

> The heart, in scripture, means desire (6:25), emotions (15:13), and thoughts (23:7). To apply the heart is to put your desires, feelings, and thoughts to get understanding. Involved in this would be: "Yea, if thou criest after knowledge, and liftest up thy voice for understanding . . ." (v. 3)

Prayer is absolutely vital! No one can apply desires, emotions, and thoughts to wisdom and understanding without the Lord's help. We are naturally inclined away from these things. That is why young people often ridicule other young people who make good grades, or who obey parents, or who try to obey the Bible. We are naturally against the very things that we need. Even a Christian will have to pray for the Lord's help. To do this, a strong desire is required . . .

> "If thou seekest her as silver, and searchest for her as for hid treasures . . ." (v. 4)

Why do people go to work every day, especially when many do not like their jobs, or do not like the people they work with; why do they go to work when they feel badly, or when the weather is bad? Everyone knows the answer: because they want that paycheck! We do many inconvenient and unpleasant things because we either want or need the money. God is saying, here, that if we had that kind of desire for wisdom, knowledge, and understanding, we would find what it means to fear the Lord and also every good path!

To recap, let us listen and remember (v. 1), lean our ears away from the world and toward God's wisdom (v. 2), pray (v. 3), and seek it every day, whether we feel like it or not (v. 4).

> "And why wilt thou, my son, be ravished with a

strange woman, and embrace the bosom of a
stranger? For the ways of man are before the eyes
of the LORD, and he pondereth all his
goings." (5:20-21)

It is a good question: why be immoral? When the world encourages it so much and even ridicules people who are faithful to husband or wife, why? There are several good reasons for being pure morally, right here in this paragraph. Faithfulness to one wife or husband is rewarded with children who are a blessing to society (v. 16), with joy (v. 18), and with satisfaction (v. 19). There is another side: we are warned that the Lord sees all that we do and ponders what He shall do about it, in v. 21. Good reasons, indeed!

All the admonitions about morality are good for both the young man and the young woman. The young man must put out much effort to avoid the immoral woman, both in person, and in pictures (which are so prevalent). The young woman should avoid the temptation to be exploited physically, whether by prostitution, or by vulgar pictures.

In the topical section of this book, you will find all the verses in Proverbs about the subject of immorality. Read them carefully and repeatedly; they show you what warning signals to beware of, and what the end result of it will be.

"A wise son maketh a glad father: but a foolish son
is the heaviness of his mother." (10:1)

For the Biblical explanation of *wise* and *foolish,* see the discussion of this verse in the chapter to Fathers.

"Better is little with the fear of the Lord than great
treasure and trouble therewith. Better is a dinner of
herbs where love is, than a stalled ox and hatred
therewith." (15: 16-17)

It is often hard for children to do without the things which other children have. We all want the latest fads and gadgets, but sometimes it is not possible. Even in a godly Christian family, things may get tight, financially. The Lord often puts even spiritual people through a time of testing. When such is true, remember that it is far better to live in a godly home where people love one another, than to have everything that others have. Many people who have "great treasure" also have much trouble! And many who have the very best food and possessions are living in a miserable family where there is much hatred. The material things of the world will never substitute for love and godliness.

" . . . A brother is born for adversity." (17:17)

One of the reasons that we have brothers and sisters is so that we can help each other during times of trouble. This is an evidence of being a born-again Christian, according to I John 3: 14-19. If we say that we are Christians but do not help our brothers and sisters, we are lying! And this should be true both of physical brothers and spiritual.

"He that begetteth a fool doeth it to his sorrow: and the father of a fool hath no joy." (17:21)

See the discussion of 10: 1 in the chapter to the Parents, for God's explanation of being a fool. The fact is, a fool is begotten; that is, we are all born with a certain amount of foolishness in us. The person who grows up to be a fool is one who never tries to overcome that sin nature. In order to overcome it, a person must be born again. "Whatsoever is born of God overcometh the world," (I John 5:4). When that born-again Christian desires the Word of God as a new baby wants milk, he grows stronger and stronger, with the happy result that he can overcome the sin nature. See I Peter 2:2.

"He that wasteth his father, and chaseth away his mother, is a son that causeth shame, and bringeth reproach." (19:26)

"Wasting his father" is the same as wasting his possessions, just as the prodigal son did, in Luke 15. He wasted his possessions on sinful living, then wound up feeding pigs to make a living, and was so poor that he wanted to eat what the pigs were eating! Proverbs has other warnings about being wasteful; here are two: "There is treasure to be desired and oil in the dwelling of the wise; but a foolish man spendeth it up." (21:20). "Whoso robbeth his father or his mother, and saith, It is no transgression; the same is the companion of a destroyer." (28:24).

It is good to learn, in youth, to save things. For instance, we should not waste food. We should take only what we plan to eat, then eat all we take. Likewise, we must be careful with our clothes and other possessions. Forming the habit of being conservative will help when one becomes an adult and has to support himself. Then he will appreciate the fact that he naturally saves, instead of wastes.

"Chasing away his mother" would be the same as forsaking her when she needs someone to take care of her. The Lord Jesus, even when He was dying, made provision for John to take care of His mother (see John 19:26-27). Does this mean it would be wrong to send parents to a nursing home? Not necessarily. In some cases, that would be the best solution, especially when there is illness and professional care is needed most of the time. But it certainly would be wrong to put them away just so they would not interfere with our plans! "Despise not thy mother when she is old," (23 :22).

If a child does waste his father and chase away his mother, that would show that the parents did not properly train him; thus, the shame and reproach. On the other hand, a child's love and care for aged parents would show that they had done the same for him.

"Cease, my son, to hear the instruction that causeth
to err from the words of knowledge." (19:27)

"The words of knowledge" are godly words, because "the fear of the LORD is the beginning of wisdom," (9: 10). Young people should reject any instruction which is opposed to God's Word. That includes the theory of evolution, knowledge about immorality, drugs, and crime, and any other matter which would contradictthe Bible.

When the Bible said "cease to hear ... " it did not mean that we should never listen to these words. That would be impossible, as long as we are in the world. We will hear some of these things everywhere we go. The idea of *hearing* is the same as obeying, as we saw in the discussion of 1:8-9. You may have to listen to some ungodly teacher deny the Bible, and you may even have to learn the material so that you can give it back on a test, but you do not have to obey it! "Cease to hear" means "stop obeying!" Christians who live in a dictatorship must endure much ungodly instruction, but many have taken their stand by refusing to obey it. "Even a child is known by his doings, whether his work be pure, and whether it be right." (20: 11)

A child will be known by his doings, not by what family he came from, or what schools he attended. A few people may be impressed with those things, but the world in general will evaluate a person by what he/she does. It is a serious mistake to depend on family to insure success.

Children should learn to work and make sure that it is a pure, right kind of work. Lam. 3:27 says, "It is good for a man that he bear the yoke in his youth." That is just another way of describing work. A child who learns to work the right kind of work will establish a good reputation, something that everyone wants. We all want to be accepted and thought well of, by someone, so much so that many will commit gross sins just to get such approval. That is unnecessary; God has shown us the way to have a good reputation, in this verse.

Children who live on farms have found it easy to learn work, but most of us live in cities where there is almost no opportunity for the kind of work that a child could do every day. Therefore, parents ought to make such opportunities available, as much as possible. Children who know the Lord should pray that He would show them some good work to do, regularly, not only for earning money, but so they can have a good testimony for Christ.

> "Whoso curseth his father or his mother, his lamp shall be put out in obscure darkness." (20:20)

Disrespect results in a severe penalty! *Lamp,* in scripture, often refers to one's reputation, that which is seen by others. See I Kings 15:4; Psa. 132: 17; and Mat. 5: 17, for examples. It also means direction, in such places as Psa. 119: 105 ("Thy word is a lamp unto my feet, and a light unto my path."); Prov. 6:23; and Rev. 2:5.

Thus, one's reputation will be destroyed and he will have no direction in life, if he curses his father and mother. A good example is the way we all react when we hear some news report about a person who has killed his parents, or other members of his family. We are all horrified! That person's reputation, no matter how good it was before, has now been destroyed. He has become a nobody.

These verses are representative of the instructions which are given to children, in Proverbs. Of course, the whole book is written to children, at one stage of life or another. It is imperative that parents do their best in teaching the young ones while they can; then it is necessary that we all, as we grow, learn all that is possible about the wisdom in this book, confidently expecting the Lord to fulfill the promises which He made to those who would obey.

Chapter 5

Proverbs - Arranged Topically

AGE
16:31
17:6
20:29

ANGER
12:16
14:17
14:29
15:1
15:18
16:14
16:32
19: 11
19:19
21:14
21:24
22:24-25
25:23
27:4
29:22
30:33

ANIMALS
6:6-8
11:22
12:10
14:4
20:2

ANIMALS
(cont.)
21:31
23:32
26:2
26:3
26:11
26:17
27:8
27:23
27:26-27
28:15
30:15
30:17
30:18-19
30:24-28
30:29-31

ATTRIBUTES OF GOD
3:12
3: 19,20
5:21
6:16
8:22
8:27-29
15:3
15:11
30:3-4

OPPRESSION
3.31-32

PRAYER
10:24
15:8
15:29
28:9

PRESERVATION OF SAINTS
2:8
2:11-12, 16
3:21-26

PRIDE & **HUMILITY**
3:7-8
3:34
6: 16-17
8:13
11:2
12:9
13:10
15:33
16:2
16:5
16:18
16:19
17:19
18: 11
18:12
20:6
26:12
29:23
30:12-13

PROSPERITY
1:32
3:9-10
4:18
8:18
10:22

PUNISHMENT
1:24-32
2:22
3:33
6:33
13:15
20:30
29:1

REBUKE
9:7-8
24:24-25
27:5

REPUTATION
10:7
22:1

THE ROD
10:13
13:24
22:15
23:13-14
26:3
29:15

SCORN
3:34

WORK
(cont.)
13:11
13:23
14:23
21:5
22:29
24:27
27:18
27:23
28:19